THE HIDDEN WORDS

OF BAHÁ'U'LLÁH

Translated by
SHOGHI EFFENDI
with the assistance of some English friends

BAHÁ'Í PUBLISHING TRUST
Wilmette, Illinois
1963

Bah aism

INTRODUCTION

Shoghi Effendi† tells in *God Passes By* how Bahá'u'lláh‡ in the year 1858 was inspired with the "gemlike utterances" which compose this book as He paced, wrapped in meditation, the banks of the Tigris. Shoghi Effendi indicates that the work is to be identified with the Hidden Book of Fatimih, which was believed to have been revealed by the Angel Gabriel through the Imam Ali for the consolation of Muhammad's grief-stricken daughter after the Prophet's death, but which has remained hidden from the world's knowledge till now made known. He describes it as "dynamic spiritual leaven cast into the life of the world for the reorientation of the minds of men, the edification of their souls and the rectification of their conduct," and ranks it as pre-eminent among the Author's ethical works.

It presents in sententious form the sum and inwardness of all the Revelations of the past. As according to prophecy all the Messengers and Prophets, including the Qaim, are gathered together beneath the shadow of the sacred standard which the Promised One has raised; so here beneath that standard is gathered their Teaching in its essence. The *Hidden Words* is not a digest, nor an ordered statement. It is a new creation. It is a distillation of Sacred Fragrances. It is a focus in which all the Great Lights of the past are joined into one Light, and all God's Yesterdays become Today.

It is given us as a single spiritual force, instinct with the presence of all the Spiritual Monarchs of the past,

---

†Shoghi Effendi, Guardian of the Bahá'í Faith, resides at the Bahá'í World Center, Haifa, Israel. 'Abdu'l-Bahá, (designated by His Father, Bahá'u'lláh as the Leader of His Faith), appointed Shoghi Effendi the first Guardian.
‡Bahá'u'lláh (1817-1892) Founder of the Bahá'í Faith, proclaimed that He was the World Messiah promised in the prophecies of all religions.

active, urgent, expansive, set now deep in the heart of man's life to effect the destined regeneration of the race.

The book appears in two parts, the first of which was originally written in Arabic, the second in Persian. The reader soon perceives that though the subject of the two sections and the manner in which the material is arranged are the same yet there are other distinctions than that of language. The Arabic part is shorter than the Persian, 19 pages as against 33; it is more simple, direct, definite, ethical, the other more personal, appealing, mystical, poetical. The Arabic verses are all addressed to 'Son' or 'Child'; the Persian addresses are greatly varied, as "O Fleeting Shadow", "O ye Dwellers in the Highest Paradise", "O Essence of Desire", "O Companion of My Throne", "O Ye Rich Ones on Earth", "O Ye Peoples of the World", "O Oppressors on Earth", "O Emigrants", "O Weed that springeth out of Dust", and many such contrasted phrases. The Arabic verses are directed to individuals, with the exception of numbers 66, 68, 69; the Persian section has thirty-three directions to groups. The approach, the tone of the Author, is different in the two parts: the writer in Arabic is a loving teacher, the writer in Persian a teaching lover. The Persian refers more often to the Manifestation as such—e.g. in verses 15, 16, 17, 23, 24, 29, 34, 35, 45, 46, 52; and to historical events of the present period, as verses 19, 63, 71. Yet the Prologue to the Arabic portion, describing the nature of the work: "this is that which hath descended from the realm of glory uttered by the tongue of power and might and revealed unto the Prophets of old . . . " applies equally to the Persian portion. And the Epilogue at the end of the Persian, applies likewise to the Arabic. And all the stanzas that make up the work, one hundred and fifty and three, are in their meaning and substance so closely interwoven and interdependent that they form one integrated whole.

ii

The *Hidden Words* is conspicuously one of those works that can only be interpreted through personal, and indeed, communal, experience. We of the spiritual twilight, who stand yet on that twilight's darker edge, we who inherit a general tradition of doubt and mammon-worship, cannot pierce the deeper meaning of these *Hidden Words* nor attain that outlook on life and the universe which it enjoins. Years and generations must pass before man can shake off the fetters he has bound upon his soul and regain that keenness of insight which he has lost through long disuse.

In its opening verse *Hidden Words* states the true and supreme aim of man's life on earth and sets forth the means by which it is to be fulfilled—the right discipline of the will and the emotions. The same goal and end were referred to by Christ in the Parable of the Talents, when the Lord said to His dutiful servant, "Thou hast been faithful over a few things, I will make thee ruler over many things".[1] Elsewhere in *Hidden Words*,[2] man's aim and hope is said to be: "to attain God's everlasting dominion and become worthy of His invisible gifts;" "to clothe the soul with that divine unity and eternity which God has made for men and thus to be to all eternity the revelation of His everlasting being;" "to recognize that man is made for God; that is, his tongue for the mention of God, his heart for God's descent upon it, his spirit to be the place of God's revelation;" "to love God that God's love may reach him;[3] that God may name his name and fill his soul with the spirit of life;" "and to enter without delay the Paradise of God's love, the heavenly home of reunion with Him." All of these goals are inward, spiritual, consisting of a particular relationship to God; and once

[1]Mat. 25:21.
[2]Arabic 2, **16**, **46**, **68**. Persian 56, **71**.
[3]Arabic 1, **4**, **6**, **64**. Persian 29, 66.

reached they are secure, certain, inalienable, eternal. The place which a man thus wins is 'ancient'; it is a part of the system of the universe and was implied in man's creation—he has at last come by effort to his own. It is in no wise material and therefore it is not subject to dissolution. It is, in the Prophet's sense, real, and therefore permanent; and nothing that is not permanent is in the teaching of the Hidden Words, worth an intelligent man's pursuit.

Nor is the objective less definite because it is expressed and explained largely through figurative language. 'Abdu'l-Bahá when asked why the Messengers speak in this manner is reported to have replied that "the revelations of the prophets can never be adequately translated owing to the poverty and imperfection of our language. Their thought is so lofty that human minds do not grasp it. Hence the use of allegories. Parables make men ponder and pray for enlightenment that they may understand the hidden meaning. Search for truth deepens man's capacity, clarifies his vision without engendering intellectual pride."

With great power and in a hundred images of great beauty The *Hidden Words* shows that this Sovereignty, Dominion, Reunion, Unity, Life, were part of the original creational Design of God; as in the Arabic verses, 3, 4, 9, 10, 11, 12, 13, 19, 32, 64, 65, and in the Persian verses 23, 27, 28, 29, 30, 34.

Telling what man is, and how he came to be, it reveals that God, while still a hidden treasure, veiled in His immemorial being and in the ancient eternity of His essence, knew His love for man, therefore He created man. Thus it was not directly His love but rather His knowledge of that love that moved God to His creative task. Which deep mystical truth finds a parallel in the direction (Arabic 10), "My love is in thee, know it"; and is more remotely reflected in the traditional ranking of the nine orders of "angels", the Seraphim holding the highest place as angels of knowledge and wisdom, the Cherubim, angels of love, the second place.

This love is man's stronghold; when he knows it and enters therein he is secure from error and from death and forever safe. He is God's lamp, made to shed the light of God Himself. He is moulded out of the clay of love and is given being out of the essence of knowledge. He is the dominion of God and will not perish; the light of God which will never be put out. God has made him to appear out of the wastes of nothingness and has ordained for his training every atom in existence and the essence of all created things. There is no peace nor rest for him save in submission before God; no cause for sorrow save distance from God nor for joy save nearness to Him. Till he loves God he remains separated from Him, far from Paradise, unsatisfied, unresting, beyond the reach of God's love. For God's home is the true believer's heart; and man's home is Reunion with God.

Bahá'u'lláh tells of the endowment and opportunities of man and calls him to action. God has made him rich and noble; He has hung upon the tree of glory for man's use the choicest fruits. God hails him with tidings of light and reunion; strengthens him with the spirit of power; leads him with the light of His countenance; summons him to the eternal; bids him magnify God's cause that God may reveal to him His greatness and that men on earth may obtain the victory; tells him man's heart is given him as a garden where he is to plant naught but the rose tree of love on which the nightingale of longing shall chant its song of rapture. He reveals that Death is a messenger of joy; and challenges him in the name of justice to be ready to forsake a thousand lives for the sake of his Great Beloved.

The soul's path to Reunion lies through love, love so all-abandoning, so complete, that it means hatred of all else save God; it means severance, detachment, purity. Christ taught that the pure in heart would have the blessedness of seeing God. The first counsel of *Hidden Words* is to possess a pure heart. Man to love God must turn away from himself; to seek God's pleasure he must not regard his own. He must glory not in his own name but in God's, must trust not in himself but in God. He will find no peace save by self-renunciation and by turning to God. Renouncing all save God he must turn his face to God's face and forgetting all save God hold communion with God. He is to seek no helper other than God; no other ever will suffice him. Nor in all the expanse of space and of heaven will he find rest anywhere save in humbleness and submission before God. The proof of true love is fortitude and patience, and the true lover yearns for tribulation as the rebel for forgiveness and the sinful for mercy. Indeed, so well content with God's good pleasure, so thankful for whatsover God ordains, must man be that he will give up all and seek a martyr's death.[4]

For man, by his constitution, has an ego, a lower self within; has a Satan, as well as an angel. Elsewhere Bahá'u'lláh speaks of him as the Essence of Error. Here in *Hidden Words* He calls man, on the one side, "O Essence of Negligence" "O Bond Slave of the World", "O Quintessence of Passion", "O Weed that Springeth out of Dust"; and on the other, "O My Brother", "O Companion of My Throne". This ego is as incompatible with the higher self as fire and water; it allies itself with God's enemy; through it man may wander away and be lost; may remain remote from God; for it drugs men to a sleep

<hr />

[4]Arabic 1, 7, 8, 15, 16, 17, 40, 45, 46, 47.

vi

of heedlessness, or calls him on a vain quest setting up a rival to God.[5]

So far has the evil principle in man hitherto prevailed over the Good that looking down the vista of the Prophetic Cycle now gone by, Bahá'u'lláh sees man by his own choice and act, impoverished and abased, busy with his own empty fancies and idle imaginings, distrusting and rebelling against God and thus destroying his hope, choosing boundless shame, binding himself in the fetters of this world and in the prison of self, bartering Paradise for the dust heap of a mortal world.[6]

Throughout the whole of the book, the subtle destructive power of the lower self is exposed and man is warned of the need of ceaseless uncompromising struggle against it in all its forms. He is bidden "turn away from thyself" . . . "there is no peace for thee save by renouncing thyself; it behoveth thee to put thy trust in Me and not in thyself." "Turn thy face unto Mine and renounce all save Me." "Forget all save Me."[7]

He who would have God, he is assured, must seek no other; he who would gaze on God's beauty must be blind to all the world. God's will and the will of another cannot dwell in one heart.[8] While the heart is defiled with desire and passion, none can commune with God. If man seeks to drink the wine of immortal life from the well-spring of detachment he must cleanse himself from the defilement of riches.[9] If the seed of divine wisdom is to spring up and grow in him, the soil of the heart in which it is planted must be pure and the seed must be watered with waters of assurance and certainty.[10] Man is warned that if in this

[5]Arabic 5, 23; Persian 16, 29, 30, 31, 33, 44, 50.
[6]Arabic 13, 14, 15, 22; Persian 21, 74.
[7]Arabic 7, 8, 15, 16.
[8]Persian 31.
[9]Persian 55.
[10]Persian 36.

Age of Justice unprecedented rewards may be gained by the truly faithful, the standards by which faith is judged are likewise heightened and the believer is bidden to strive that his deeds may be cleansed from the dust of self and hypocrisy and find favor at the court of glory, since the Assayers of Mankind will now in the holy presence of the Adored One accept naught but absolute virtue and deeds of stainless purity.

The quelling of this ego, the severance from selfish desires is indeed the essential task that confronts the aspiring soul. The final challenge to the faithful with which Bahá'u'lláh closes this ethical work is: "Let it now be seen what your endeavors in the path of detachment will reveal". The Creator has left this imperfection in man's constitution and given him freedom of will to strive against it in order that man may, through his own endeavor, "become worthy to meet Me (God) and to mirror forth My Beauty". Were not the ego there man could not earn praise and reward; he might be spared test and trial but he would be a mere automaton. This demand for effort, this privilege of free choice, may make this planet a place of torment but it makes earth-life a field of possible victory, an arena where moral attainment is really a man's own deed, won under the beneficent law of justice by his own knowledge, determination, and action. In the "next world" this opportunity of achieving worthiness is not given. Man, for his advancement there depends not on self-effort and justice but on God's mercy. Therefore Bahá'u'lláh counsels man to seize the opportunity here and now, for it will come to him no more. The fires of hell, it is explained elsewhere, are the sense of priceless opportunities thrown away and now lost forever.

The *Hidden Words* stands as a sign of God's victory and of the fulfillment of His ancient purpose for mankind. No book radiant with such intensity of light has ever been given or could have been given to mankind before. It contains the whole sum of all Revelations rounding to their completeness, renewed in power, and brought to the perfection of unity by the crowning words of Bahá'u'lláh. It is the Badge of the oneness of all the Prophets of East and West from the beginning until now; the Badge of that Universal Faith on which shall be built the Most Great Peace.

GEORGE TOWNSHEND

THE HIDDEN WORDS OF BAHÁ'U'LLÁH

Part I.—From the Arabic

HE IS THE GLORY OF GLORIES

This is that which hath descended from the realm of glory, uttered by the tongue of power and might, and revealed unto the Prophets of old. We have taken the inner essence thereof and clothed it in the garment of brevity, as a token of grace unto the righteous, that they may stand faithful unto the Covenant of God, may fulfill in their lives His trust, and in the realm of spirit obtain the gem of Divine virtue.

1. O SON OF SPIRIT!

   My first counsel is this: Possess a pure, kindly and radiant heart, that thine may be a sovereignty ancient, imperishable and everlasting.

2. O SON OF SPIRIT!

   The best beloved of all things in My sight is Justice; turn not away therefrom if thou desirest

Me, and neglect it not that I may confide in thee. By its aid thou shalt see with thine own eyes and not through the eyes of others, and shalt know of thine own knowledge and not through the knowledge of thy neighbor. Ponder this in thy heart; how it behooveth thee to be. Verily justice is My gift to thee and the sign of My loving-kindness. Set it then before thine eyes.

3. O SON OF MAN!

Veiled in My immemorial being and in the ancient eternity of My essence, I knew My love for thee; therefore I created thee, have engraved on thee Mine image and revealed to thee My beauty.

4. O SON OF MAN!

I loved thy creation, hence I created thee. Wherefore, do thou love Me, that I may name thy name and fill thy soul with the spirit of life.

5. O SON OF BEING!

Love Me, that I may love thee. If thou lovest Me not, My love can in no wise reach thee. Know this, O servant.

6. O SON OF BEING!

Thy Paradise is My love; thy heavenly home, reunion with Me. Enter therein and tarry not. This is that which hath been destined for thee in Our kingdom above and Our exalted dominion.

7. O SON OF MAN!

If thou lovest Me, turn away from thyself; and if thou seekest My pleasure, regard not thine own; that thou mayest die in Me and I may eternally live in thee.

8. O SON OF SPIRIT!

There is no peace for thee save by renouncing thyself and turning unto Me; for it behooveth thee to glory in My name, not in thine own; to put thy trust in Me and not in thyself, since I desire to be loved alone and above all that is.

9. O SON OF BEING!

My love is My stronghold; he that entereth therein is safe and secure, and he that turneth away shall surely stray and perish.

10. O SON OF UTTERANCE!

Thou art My stronghold; enter therein that thou mayest abide in safety. My love is in thee, know it, that thou mayest find Me near unto thee.

11. O SON OF BEING!

Thou art My lamp and My light is in thee. Get thou from it thy radiance and seek none other than Me. For I have created thee rich and have bountifully shed My favor upon thee.

12. O SON OF BEING!

With the hands of power I made thee and with the fingers of strength I created thee; and within thee have I placed the essence of My light. Be thou content with it and seek naught else, for My work is perfect and My command is binding. Question it not, nor have a doubt thereof.

13. O SON OF SPIRIT!

I created thee rich, why dost thou bring thyself down to poverty? Noble I made thee, wherewith dost thou abase thyself? Out of the essence of knowledge I gave thee being, why seekest thou enlightenment from anyone beside Me? Out of the clay of love I molded thee, how dost thou busy thyself with another? Turn thy sight unto thyself, that thou mayest find Me standing within thee, mighty, powerful and self-subsisting.

14. O SON OF MAN!

Thou art My dominion and My dominion perisheth not, wherefore fearest thou thy perishing? Thou art My light and My light shall never be extinguished, why dost thou dread extinction? Thou art My glory and My glory fadeth not; thou art My robe and My robe shall never be outworn. Abide then in thy love for Me, that thou mayest find Me in the realm of glory.

15. O SON OF UTTERANCE!

Turn thy face unto Mine and renounce all save Me; for My sovereignty endureth and My dominion perisheth not. If thou seekest another than Me, yea, if thou searchest the universe for evermore, thy quest will be in vain.

16. O SON OF LIGHT!

Forget all save Me and commune with My spirit. This is of the essence of My command, therefore turn unto it.

17. O SON OF MAN!

Be thou content with Me and seek no other helper. For none but Me can ever suffice thee.

18. O SON OF SPIRIT!

Ask not of Me that which We desire not for thee, then be content with what We have ordained for thy sake, for this is that which profiteth thee, if therewith thou dost content thyself.

19. O SON OF THE WONDROUS VISION!

I have breathed within thee a breath of My own Spirit, that thou mayest be My lover. Why hast thou forsaken Me and sought a beloved other than Me?

20. O SON OF SPIRIT!

My claim on thee is great, it cannot be forgotten. My grace to thee is plenteous, it cannot be veiled. My love has made in thee its home, it cannot be concealed. My light is manifest to thee, it cannot be obscured.

21. O SON OF MAN!

Upon the tree of effulgent glory I have hung for thee the choicest fruits, wherefore hast thou turned away and contented thyself with that which is less good? Return then unto that which is better for thee in the realm on high.

22. O SON OF SPIRIT!

Noble have I created thee, yet thou hast abased thyself. Rise then unto that for which thou wast created.

23. O SON OF THE SUPREME!

To the eternal I call thee, yet thou dost seek that which perisheth. What hath made thee turn away from Our desire and seek thine own?

24. O SON OF MAN!

Transgress not thy limits, nor claim that which beseemeth thee not. Prostrate thyself before the countenance of thy God, the Lord of might and power.

25. O SON OF SPIRIT!

Vaunt not thyself over the poor, for I lead him on his way and behold thee in thy evil plight and confound thee for evermore.

26. O SON OF BEING!

How couldst thou forget thine own faults and busy thyself with the faults of others? Whoso doeth this is accursed of Me.

27. O SON OF MAN!

Breathe not the sins of others so long as thou art thyself a sinner. Shouldst thou transgress this command, accursed wouldst thou be, and to this I bear witness.

28. O SON OF SPIRIT!

Know thou of a truth: He that biddeth men be just and himself committeth iniquity is not of Me, even though he bear My name.

29. O SON OF BEING!

Ascribe not to any soul that which thou wouldst not have ascribed to thee, and say not that which thou doest not. This is My command unto thee, do thou observe it.

30. O SON OF MAN!

Deny not My servant should he ask anything from thee, for his face is My face; be then abashed before Me.

31. O SON OF BEING!

Bring thyself to account each day ere thou art summoned to a reckoning; for death, unheralded, shall come upon thee and thou shalt be called to give account for thy deeds.

32. O SON OF THE SUPREME!

I have made death a messenger of joy to thee. Wherefore dost thou grieve? I made the light to shed on thee its splendor. Why dost thou veil thyself therefrom?

33. O SON OF SPIRIT!

With the joyful tidings of light I hail thee: rejoice! To the court of holiness I summon thee; abide therein that thou mayest live in peace for evermore.

34. O SON OF SPIRIT!

The spirit of holiness beareth unto thee the joyful tidings of reunion; wherefore dost thou grieve? The spirit of power confirmeth thee in His cause; why dost thou veil thyself? The light of His countenance doth lead thee; how canst thou go astray?

35. **O SON OF MAN!**

Sorrow not save that thou art far from Us. Rejoice not save that thou art drawing near and returning unto Us.

36. **O SON OF MAN!**

Rejoice in the gladness of thine heart, that thou mayest be worthy to meet Me and to mirror forth My beauty.

37. **O SON OF MAN!**

Divest not thyself of My beauteous robe, and forfeit not thy portion from My wondrous fountain, lest thou shouldst thirst for evermore.

38. **O SON OF BEING!**

Walk in My statutes for love of Me and deny thyself that which thou desirest if thou seekest My pleasure.

39. O SON OF MAN!

Neglect not My commandments if thou lovest My beauty, and forget not My counsels if thou wouldst attain My good pleasure.

40. O SON OF MAN!

Wert thou to speed through the immensity of space and traverse the expanse of heaven, yet thou wouldst find no rest save in submission to Our command and humbleness before Our Face.

41. O SON OF MAN!

Magnify My cause that I may reveal unto thee the mysteries of My greatness and shine upon thee with the light of eternity.

42. O SON OF MAN!

Humble thyself before Me, that I may graciously visit thee. Arise for the triumph of My cause, that while yet on earth thou mayest obtain the victory.

43. O SON OF BEING!

Make mention of Me on My earth, that in My heaven I may remember thee, thus shall Mine eyes and thine be solaced.

44. O SON OF THE THRONE!

Thy hearing is My hearing, hear thou therewith. Thy sight is My sight, do thou see therewith, that in thine inmost soul thou mayest testify unto My exalted sanctity, and I within Myself may bear witness unto an exalted station for thee.

45. O SON OF BEING!

Seek a martyr's death in My path, content with My pleasure and thankful for that which I ordain, that thou mayest repose with Me beneath the canopy of majesty behind the tabernacle of glory.

46. O SON OF MAN!

Ponder and reflect. Is it thy wish to die upon thy bed, or to shed thy life-blood on the dust, a martyr in My path, and so become the manifestation of My command and the revealer of My light in the highest paradise? Judge thou aright, O servant!

47. O SON OF MAN!

By My beauty! To tinge thy hair with thy blood is greater in My sight than the creation of the universe and the light of both worlds. Strive then to attain this, O servant!

48. O SON OF MAN!

For everything there is a sign. The sign of love is fortitude under My decree and patience under My trials.

49. O SON OF MAN!

The true lover yearneth for tribulation even as doth the rebel for forgiveness and the sinful for mercy.

50. O SON OF MAN!

If adversity befall thee not in My path, how canst thou walk in the ways of them that are content with My pleasure? If trials afflict thee not in thy longing to meet Me, how wilt thou attain the light in thy love for My beauty?

51. O SON OF MAN!

My calamity is My providence, outwardly it is fire and vengeance, but inwardly it is light and mercy. Hasten thereunto that thou mayest become an eternal light and an immortal spirit. This is My command unto thee, do thou observe it.

52. O SON OF MAN!

Should prosperity befall thee, rejoice not, and should abasement come upon thee, grieve not, for both shall pass away and be no more.

53. O SON OF BEING!

If poverty overtake thee, be not sad; for in time the Lord of wealth shall visit thee. Fear not abasement, for glory shall one day rest on thee.

54. O SON OF BEING!

If thine heart be set upon this eternal, imperishable dominion, and this ancient, everlasting life, forsake this mortal and fleeting sovereignty.

55. O SON OF BEING!

Busy not thyself with this world, for with fire We test the gold, and with gold We test Our servants.

56. O SON OF MAN!

Thou dost wish for gold and I desire thy freedom from it. Thou thinkest thyself rich in its possession, and I recognize thy wealth in thy sanctity therefrom. By My life! This is My knowledge, and that is thy fancy; how can My way accord with thine?

57. O SON OF MAN!

Bestow My wealth upon My poor, that in heaven thou mayest draw from stores of unfading splendor and treasures of imperishable glory. But by My life! To offer up thy soul is a more glorious thing couldst thou but see with Mine eye.

58. O SON OF MAN!

The temple of being is My throne; cleanse it of all things, that there I may be established and there I may abide.

59. O SON OF BEING!

Thy heart is My home; sanctify it for My descent. Thy spirit is My place of revelation; cleanse it for My manifestation.

60. O SON OF MAN!

Put thy hand into My bosom, that I may rise above thee, radiant and resplendent.

61. O SON OF MAN!

Ascend unto My heaven, that thou mayest obtain the joy of reunion, and from the chalice of imperishable glory quaff the peerless wine.

62. O SON OF MAN!

Many a day hath passed over thee whilst thou hast busied thyself with thy fancies and idle imaginings. How long art thou to slumber on thy bed? Lift up thy head from slumber, for the Sun hath risen to the zenith, haply it may shine upon thee with the light of beauty.

63. O SON OF MAN!

The light hath shone on thee from the horizon of the sacred Mount and the spirit of enlightenment hath breathed in the Sinai of thy heart. Wherefore, free thyself from the veils of idle fancies and enter into My court, that thou mayest be fit for everlasting life and worthy to meet Me. Thus may death not come upon thee, neither weariness nor trouble.

64. O SON OF MAN!

My eternity is My creation, I have created it for thee. Make it the garment of thy temple.

My unity is My handiwork; I have wrought it for thee; clothe thyself therewith, that thou mayest be to all eternity the revelation of My everlasting being.

65. O SON OF MAN!

My majesty is My gift to thee, and My grandeur the token of My mercy unto thee. That which beseemeth Me none shall understand, nor can any one recount. Verily, I have preserved it in My hidden storehouses and in the treasuries of My command, as a sign of My lovingkindness unto My servants and My mercy unto My people.

66. O CHILDREN OF THE DIVINE AND INVISIBLE ESSENCE!

Ye shall be hindered from loving Me and souls shall be perturbed as they make mention of Me. For minds cannot grasp Me nor hearts contain Me.

67. O SON OF BEAUTY!

By My spirit and by My favor! By My mercy and by My beauty! All that I have revealed unto thee with the tongue of power, and have written for thee with the pen of might, hath been in accordance with thy capacity and understanding, not with My state and the melody of My voice.

68. O CHILDREN OF MEN!

Know ye not why We created you all from the same dust? That no one should exalt himself over the other. Ponder at all times in your hearts how ye were created. Since We have created you all from one same substance it is incumbent on you to be even as one soul, to walk with the same feet, eat with the same mouth and dwell in the same land, that from your inmost being, by your deeds and actions, the signs of oneness and the essence of detachment may be made manifest. Such is My counsel to you, O concourse of light! Heed ye this counsel that ye may obtain the fruit of holiness from the tree of wondrous glory.

69. O YE SONS OF SPIRIT!

Ye are My treasury, for in you I have treasured the pearls of My mysteries and the gems of My knowledge. Guard them from the strangers amidst My servants and from the ungodly amongst My people.

ɔ. O SON OF HIM THAT STOOD BY HIS
   OWN ENTITY IN THE KINGDOM OF
   HIS SELF!

Know thou, that I have wafted unto thee all
the fragrances of holiness, have fully revealed
to thee My word, have perfected through thee
My bounty and have desired for thee that which
I have desired for My Self.   Be then content
with My pleasure and thankful unto Me.

ɪ. O SON OF MAN!

Write all that We have revealed unto thee with
the ink of light upon the tablet of thy spirit.
Should this not be in thy power, then make
thine ink of the essence of thy heart.   If this
thou canst not do, then write with that crimson
ink that hath been shed in My path.   Sweeter
indeed is this to Me than all else, that its light
may endure for ever.

THE HIDDEN WORDS
OF BAHÁ'U'LLÁH

Part II.—*From the Persian*

In the Name of the Lord of Utterance, Th
Mighty.

1. O YE PEOPLE THAT HAVE MINDS T(
   KNOW AND EARS TO HEAR!

The first call of the Beloved is this: O mysti
nightingale! Abide not but in the rose-garde
of the spirit. O messenger of the Solomon o
love! Seek thou no shelter except in the Sheb;
of the well-beloved, and O immortal phœnix
dwell not save on the mount of faithfulness
Therein is thy habitation, if on the wings of th'
soul thou soarest to the realm of the infinit
and seekest to attain thy goal.

2. O SON OF SPIRIT!

The bird seeketh its nest; the nightingale th
charm of the rose; whilst those birds, the heart;
of men, content with transient dust, hav

strayed far from their eternal nest, and with
eyes turned towards the slough of heedlessness
are bereft of the glory of the divine presence.
Alas! How strange and pitiful; for a mere cup-
ful, they have turned away from the billowing
seas of the Most High, and remained far from
the most effulgent horizon.

3. O FRIEND!

In the garden of thy heart plant naught but
the rose of love, and from the nightingale of
affection and desire loosen not thy hold. Treasure the companionship of the righteous and
eschew all fellowship with the ungodly.

4. O SON OF JUSTICE!

Whither can a lover go but to the land of his
beloved? and what seeker findeth rest away
from his heart's desire? To the true lover reunion is life, and separation is death. His
breast is void of patience and his heart hath no
peace. A myriad lives he would forsake to
hasten to the abode of his beloved.

5. O SON OF DUST!

Verily I say unto thee: Of all men the most
negligent is he that disputeth idly and seeketh

to advance himself over his brother. Say, ❨
brethren! Let deeds, not words, be your adorn
ing.

6. O SON OF EARTH!

Know, verily, the heart wherein the least rem
nant of envy yet lingers, shall never attain M
everlasting dominion, nor inhale the swee
savors of holiness breathing from My kingdor
of sanctity.

7. O SON OF LOVE!

Thou art but one step away from the gloriou
heights above and from the celestial tree o
love. Take thou one pace and with the nex
advance into the immortal realm and enter th
pavilion of eternity. Give ear then to tha
which hath been revealed by the pen of glory

8. O SON OF GLORY!

Be swift in the path of holiness, and enter th
heaven of communion with Me. Cleanse th
heart with the burnish of the spirit, and hastei
to the court of the Most High.

9. O FLEETING SHADOW!

Pass beyond the baser stages of doubt and rise to the exalted heights of certainty. Open the eye of truth, that thou mayest behold the veilless Beauty and exclaim: Hallowed be the Lord, the most excellent of all creators!

10. O SON OF DESIRE!

Give ear unto this: Never shall mortal eye recognise the everlasting beauty, nor the lifeless heart delight in aught but in the withered bloom. For like seeketh like, and taketh pleasure in the company of its kind.

11. O SON OF DUST!

Blind thine eyes, that thou mayest behold My beauty; stop thine ears, that thou mayest hearken unto the sweet melody of My voice; empty thyself of all learning, that thou mayest partake of My knowledge; and sanctify thyself from riches, that thou mayest obtain a lasting share from the ocean of My eternal wealth. Blind thine eyes, that is, to all save My beauty; stop thine ears to all save My word; empty thyself of all learning save the knowledge of Me; that with a clear vision, a pure heart and an attentive ear thou mayest enter the court of My holiness.

12. O MAN OF TWO VISIONS!

Close one eye and open the other. Close one to the world and all that is therein, and open the other to the hallowed beauty of the Beloved.

13. O MY CHILDREN!

I fear lest, bereft of the melody of the dove of heaven, ye will sink back to the shades of utter loss, and, never having gazed upon the beauty of the rose, return to water and clay.

14. O FRIENDS!

Abandon not the everlasting beauty for a beauty that must die, and set not your affections on this mortal world of dust.

15. O SON OF SPIRIT!

The time cometh, when the nightingale of holiness will no longer unfold the inner mysteries and ye will all be bereft of the celestial melody and of the voice from on high.

16. O ESSENCE OF NEGLIGENCE!

Myriads of mystic tongues find utterance in one speech, and myriads of hidden mysteries are revealed in a single melody; yet, alas, there is no ear to hear, nor heart to understand.

17. O COMRADES!

The gates that open on the Placeless stand wide and the habitation of the loved one is adorned with the lovers' blood, yet all but a few remain bereft of this celestial city, and even of these few, none but the smallest handful hath been found with a pure heart and sanctified spirit.

18. O YE DWELLERS IN THE HIGHEST PARADISE!

Proclaim unto the children of assurance that within the realms of holiness, nigh unto the celestial paradise, a new garden hath appeared, round which circle the denizens of the realm on high and the immortal dwellers of the exalted paradise. Strive, then, that ye may attain that station, that ye may unravel the mysteries of love from its wind-flowers and learn the secret of divine and consummate wisdom from its eternal fruits. Solaced are the eyes of them that enter and abide therein!

19. O MY FRIENDS!

Have ye forgotten that true and radiant morn, when in those hallowed and blessed surroundings ye were all gathered in My presence beneath the shade of the tree of life, which is planted in the all-glorious paradise? Awe-struck ye listened as I gave utterance to these three most holy words: O friends! Prefer not your will to Mine, never desire that which I have not desired for you, and approach Me not with lifeless hearts, defiled with worldly desires and cravings. Would ye but sanctify your souls, ye would at this present hour recall that place and those surroundings, and the truth of My utterance should be made evident unto all of you.

In the eighth of the most holy lines, in the fifth Tablet of Paradise, He saith:

20. O YE THAT ARE LYING AS DEAD ON THE COUCH OF HEEDLESSNESS!

Ages have passed and your precious lives are well-nigh ended, yet not a single breath of purity hath reached Our court of holiness from you. Though immersed in the ocean of misbelief, yet with your lips ye profess the one true faith of God. Him whom I abhor ye have loved, and of My foe ye have made a friend. Notwithstanding, ye walk on My earth complacent and self-satisfied, heedless that My earth is weary of you and everything within it shunneth you. Were ye but to open your eyes, ye would, in truth, prefer a myriad griefs unto this joy, and would count death itself better than this life.

21. O MOVING FORM OF DUST!

I desire communion with thee, but thou wouldst put no trust in Me. The sword of thy rebellion hath felled the tree of thy hope. At all times I am near unto thee, but thou art ever far from Me. Imperishable glory I have chosen for thee, yet boundless shame thou hast chosen for thyself. While there is yet time, return, and lose not thy chance.

22. O SON OF DESIRE!

The learned and the wise have for long years striven and failed to attain the presence of the All-Glorious; they have spent their lives in search of Him, yet did not behold the beauty of His countenance. Thou without the least effort didst attain thy goal, and without search hast obtained the object of thy quest. Yet, notwithstanding, thou didst remain so wrapt in the veil of self, that thine eyes beheld not the beauty of the Beloved, nor did thy hand touch the hem of His robe. Ye that have eyes, behold and wonder.

23. O DWELLERS IN THE CITY OF LOVE!

Mortal blasts have beset the everlasting candle, and the beauty of the celestial Youth is veiled in the darkness of dust. The chief of the monarchs of love is wronged by the people of tyranny and the dove of holiness lies prisoned in the talons of owls. The dwellers in the pavilion of glory and the celestial concourse bewail and lament, while ye repose in the realm of negligence, and esteem yourselves as of the true friends. How vain are your imaginings!

24. O YE THAT ARE FOOLISH, YET HAVE A NAME TO BE WISE!

Wherefore do ye wear the guise of shepherds, when inwardly ye have become wolves, intent upon My flock? Ye are even as the star, which riseth ere the dawn, and which, though it seem radiant and luminous, leadeth the wayfarers of My city astray into the paths of perdition.

25. O YE SEEMING FAIR YET INWARDLY FOUL!

Ye are like clear but bitter water, which to outward seeming is crystal pure but of which, when tested by the divine Assayer, not a drop is accepted. Yea, the sun beam falls alike upon the dust and the mirror, yet differ they in reflection even as doth the star from the earth: nay, immeasurable is the difference!

26. O MY FRIEND IN WORD!

Ponder awhile. Hast thou ever heard that friend and foe should abide in one heart? Cast out then the stranger, that the Friend may enter His home.

27. O SON OF DUST!

All that is in heaven and earth I have ordained for thee, except the human heart, which I have made the habitation of My beauty and glory; yet thou didst give My home and dwelling to another than Me; and whenever the manifestation of My holiness sought His own abode, a stranger found He there, and, homeless, hastened unto the sanctuary of the Beloved. Notwithstanding I have concealed thy secret and desired not thy shame.

28. O ESSENCE OF DESIRE!

At many a dawn have I turned from the realms of the Placeless unto thine abode, and found thee on the bed of ease busied with others than Myself. Thereupon, even as the flash of the spirit, I returned to the realms of celestial glory and breathed it not in My retreats above unto the hosts of holiness.

29. O SON OF BOUNTY!

Out of the wastes of nothingness, with the clay of My command I made thee to appear, and have ordained for thy training every atom in existence and the essence of all created things. Thus, ere thou didst issue from thy mother's womb, I destined for thee two founts of gleaming milk, eyes to watch over thee, and hearts to love thee. Out of My loving-kindness, 'neath the shade of My mercy I nurtured thee, and guarded thee by the essence of My grace and favor. And My purpose in all this was that thou mightest attain My everlasting dominion and become worthy of My invisible bestowals. And yet heedless thou didst remain, and when fully grown, thou didst neglect all My bounties and occupied thyself with thine idle imaginings, in such wise that thou didst become wholly forgetful, and, turning away from the portals of the Friend didst abide within the courts of My enemy.

30. O BOND SLAVE OF THE WORLD!

Many a dawn hath the breeze of My loving-kindness wafted over thee and found thee upon the bed of heedlessness fast asleep. Bewailing then thy plight it returned whence it came.

31. O SON OF EARTH!

Wouldst thou have Me, seek none other than Me; and wouldst thou gaze upon My beauty, close thine eyes to the world and all that is therein; for My will and the will of another than Me, even as fire and water, cannot dwell together in one heart.

32. O BEFRIENDED STRANGER!

The candle of thine heart is lighted by the hand of My power, quench it not with the contrary winds of self and passion. The healer of all thine ills is remembrance of Me, forget it not. Make My love thy treasure and cherish it even as thy very sight and life.

33. O MY BROTHER!

Hearken to the delightsome words of My honeyed tongue, and quaff the stream of mystic holiness from My sugar-shedding lips. Sow the

seeds of My divine wisdom in the pure soil of
thy heart, and water them with the water of
certitude, that the hyacinths of My knowledge
and wisdom may spring up fresh and green in
the sacred city of thy heart.

34. O DWELLERS OF MY PARADISE!

With the hands of loving-kindness I have
planted in the holy garden of paradise the young
tree of your love and friendship, and have
watered it with the goodly showers of My tender
grace; now that the hour of its fruiting is come,
strive that it may be protected, and be not con-
sumed with the flame of desire and passion.

35. O MY FRIENDS!

Quench ye the lamp of error, and kindle within
your hearts the everlasting torch of divine guidance. For ere long the assayers of mankind
shall, in the holy presence of the Adored, accept
naught but purest virtue and deeds of stainless
holiness.

36. O SON OF DUST!

The wise are they that speak not unless they
obtain a hearing, even as the cup-bearer, who

proffereth not his cup till he findeth a seeker, and the lover who crieth not out from the depths of his heart until he gazeth upon the beauty of his beloved. Wherefore sow the seeds of wisdom and knowledge in the pure soil of the heart, and keep them hidden, till the hyacinths of divine wisdom spring from the heart and not from mire and clay.

In the first line of the Tablet it is recorded and written, and within the sanctuary of the tabernacle of God is hidden:

37. O MY SERVANT!

Abandon not for that which perisheth an everlasting dominion, and cast not away celestial sovereignty for a worldly desire. This is the river of everlasting life that hath flowed from the well-spring of the pen of the merciful; well is it with them that drink!

38. O SON OF SPIRIT!

Burst thy cage asunder, and even as the phœnix of love soar into the firmament of holiness. Renounce thyself and, filled with the spirit of mercy, abide in the realm of celestial sanctity.

39. O OFFSPRING OF DUST!

Be not content with the ease of a passing day, and deprive not thyself of everlasting rest. Barter not the garden of eternal delight for the dust-heap of a mortal world. Up from thy prison ascend unto the glorious meads above, and from thy mortal cage wing thy flight unto the paradise of the Placeless.

40. O MY SERVANT!

Free thyself from the fetters of this world, and loose thy soul from the prison of self. Seize thy chance, for it will come to thee no more.

41. O SON OF MY HANDMAID!

Didst thou behold immortal sovereignty, thou wouldst strive to pass from this fleeting world. But to conceal the one from thee and to reveal the other is a mystery which none but the pure in heart can comprehend.

42. O MY SERVANT!

Purge thy heart from malice and, innocent of envy, enter the divine court of holiness.

43. O MY FRIENDS!

Walk ye in the ways of the good pleasure of the Friend, and know that His pleasure is in the pleasure of His creatures. That is: no man should enter the house of his friend save at his friend's pleasure, nor lay hands upon his treasures nor prefer his own will to his friend's, and in no wise seek an advantage over him. Ponder this, ye that have insight!

44. O COMPANION OF MY THRONE!

Hear no evil, and see no evil, abase not thyself, neither sigh and weep. Speak no evil, that thou mayest not hear it spoken unto thee, and magnify not the faults of others that thine own faults may not appear great; and wish not the abasement of anyone, that thine own abasement be not exposed. Live then the days of thy life, that are less than a fleeting moment, with thy mind stainless, thy heart unsullied, thy thoughts pure, and thy nature sanctified, so that, free and content, thou mayest put away this mortal frame, and repair unto the mystic paradise and abide in the eternal kingdom for evermore.

45. ALAS! ALAS! O LOVERS OF WORLDLY DESIRE!

Even as the swiftness of lightning ye have passed by the Beloved One, and have set your hearts on satanic fancies. Ye bow the knee before your vain imagining, and call it truth. Ye turn your eyes towards the thorn, and name it a flower. Not a pure breath have ye breathed, nor hath the breeze of detachment been wafted from the meadows of your hearts. Ye have cast to the winds the loving counsels of the Beloved and have effaced them utterly from the tablet of your hearts, and even as the beasts of the field, ye move and have your being within the pastures of desire and passion.

46. O BRETHREN IN THE PATH!

Wherefore have ye neglected the mention of the Loved One, and kept remote from His holy presence? The essence of beauty is within the peerless pavilion, set upon the throne of glory, whilst ye busy yourselves with idle contentions. The sweet savors of holiness are breathing and the breath of bounty is wafted, yet ye are all sorely afflicted and deprived thereof. Alas for you and for them that walk in your ways and follow in your footsteps!

47. O CHILDREN OF DESIRE!

Put away the garment of vainglory, and divest yourselves of the attire of haughtiness.

In the third of the most holy lines writ and recorded in the Ruby Tablet by the pen of the unseen this is revealed:

48. O BRETHREN!

Be forbearing one with another and set not your affections on things below. Pride not yourselves in your glory, and be not ashamed of abasement. By My beauty! I have created all things from dust, and to dust will I return them again.

49. O CHILDREN OF DUST!

Tell the rich of the midnight sighing of the poor, lest heedlessness lead them into the path of destruction, and deprive them of the Tree of Wealth. To give and to be generous are attributes of Mine; well is it with him that adorneth himself with My virtues.

50. O QUINTESSENCE OF PASSION!

Put away all covetousness and seek contentment; for the covetous hath ever been deprived, and the contented hath ever been loved and praised.

51. O SON OF MY HANDMAID!

Be not troubled in poverty nor confident in
riches, for poverty is followed by riches, and
riches are followed by poverty. Yet to be poor
in all save God is a wondrous gift, belittle not
the value thereof, for in the end it will make
thee rich in God, and thus thou shalt know the
meaning of the utterance, " In truth ye are the
poor," and the holy words, " God is the all-
possessing," shall even as the true morn break
forth gloriously resplendent upon the horizon
of the lover's heart, and abide secure on the
throne of wealth.

52. O CHILDREN OF NEGLIGENCE AND PASSION!

Ye have suffered My enemy to enter My house
and have cast out My friend, for ye have en-
shrined the love of another than Me in your
hearts. Give ear to the sayings of the Friend
and turn towards His paradise. Worldly
friends, seeking their own good, appear to love
one the other, whereas the true Friend hath
loved and doth love you for your own sakes;
indeed He hath suffered for your guidance count-
less afflictions. Be not disloyal to such a Friend,
nay rather hasten unto Him. Such is the day-
star of the word of truth and faithfulness, that

hath dawned above the horizon of the pen of the Lord of all names. Open your ears that ye may hearken unto the word of God, the help in peril, the self-existent.

53. O YE THAT PRIDE YOURSELVES ON MORTAL RICHES!

Know ye in truth that wealth is a mighty barrier between the seeker and his desire, the lover and his beloved. The rich, but for a few, shall in no wise attain the court of His presence nor enter the city of content and resignation. Well is it then with him, who, being rich, is not hindered by his riches from the eternal kingdom, nor deprived by them of imperishable dominion. By the most great name! The splendor of such a wealthy man shall illuminate the dwellers of heaven even as the sun enlightens the people of the earth!

54. O YE RICH ONES ON EARTH!

The poor in your midst are My trust; guard ye My trust, and be not intent only on your own ease.

55. O SON OF PASSION!

Cleanse thyself from the defilement of riches and in perfect peace advance into the realm of poverty; that from the well-spring of detachment thou mayest quaff the wine of immortal life.

56. O MY SON!

The company of the ungodly increaseth sorrow, whilst fellowship with the righteous cleanseth the rust from off the heart. He that seeketh to commune with God, let him betake himself to the companionship of His loved ones; and he that desireth to hearken unto the word of God, let him give ear to the words of His chosen ones.

57. O SON OF DUST!

Beware! Walk not with the ungodly and seek not fellowship with him, for such companionship turneth the radiance of the heart into infernal fire.

58. O SON OF MY HANDMAID!

Wouldst thou seek the grace of the Holy Spirit, enter into fellowship with the righteous, for he hath drunk the cup of eternal life at the hands of the immortal Cup-bearer and even as the true morn doth quicken and illumine the hearts of the dead.

59. O HEEDLESS ONES!

Think not the secrets of hearts are hidden, nay, know ye of a certainty that in clear characters they are engraved and are openly manifest in the holy Presence.

60. O FRIENDS!

Verily I say, whatsoever ye have concealed within your hearts is to Us open and manifest as the day; but that it is hidden is of Our grace and favor, and not of your deserving.

61. O SON OF MAN!

A dewdrop out of the fathomless ocean of My mercy I have shed upon the peoples of the world, yet found none turn thereunto, inasmuch as every one hath turned away from the celestial wine of unity unto the foul dregs of impurity, and, content with mortal cup, hath put away the chalice of immortal beauty. Vile is that wherewith he is contented.

62. O SON OF DUST!

Turn not away thine eyes from the matchless wine of the immortal Beloved, and open them not to foul and mortal dregs. Take from the hands of the divine Cup-bearer the chalice of immortal life, that all wisdom may be thine, and that thou mayest hearken unto the mystic voice calling from the realm of the invisible. Cry aloud, ye that are of low aim! Wherefore have ye turned away from My holy and immortal wine unto evanescent water?

63. O YE PEOPLES OF THE WORLD!

Know verily that an unforeseen calamity is following you and that grievous retribution awaiteth you. Think not the deeds ye have committed have been blotted from My sight. By My beauty! All your doings hath My pen graven with open characters upon tablets of chrysolite.

64. O OPPRESSORS ON EARTH!

Withdraw your hands from tyranny, for I have pledged Myself not to forgive any man's injustice. This is My covenant which I have irrevocably decreed in the preserved tablet and sealed it with My seal of glory.

65. O REBELLIOUS ONES!

My forbearance hath emboldened you and My long-suffering hath made you negligent, in such wise that ye have spurred on the fiery charger of passion into perilous ways that lead unto destruction. Have ye thought Me heedless or that I was unaware?

66. O EMIGRANTS!

The tongue I have designed for the mention of Me, defile it not with detraction. If the fire of self overcome you, remember your own faults and not the faults of My creatures, inasmuch as every one of you knoweth his own self better than he knoweth others.

67. O CHILDREN OF FANCY!

Know verily, that while the radiant dawn breaketh above the horizon of eternal holiness, the satanic secrets and deeds done in the gloom of night shall be laid bare and manifest before the peoples of the world.

68. O WEED THAT SPRINGETH OUT OF DUST!

Wherefore have not these soiled hands of thine touched first thine own garment, and why with thine heart defiled with desire and passion dost thou seek to commune with Me and to enter My sacred realm? Far, far are ye from that which ye desire.

69. O CHILDREN OF ADAM!

Holy words and pure and goodly deeds ascend unto the heaven of celestial glory. Strive that your deeds may be cleansed from the dust of self and hypocrisy and find favor at the court of glory; for ere long the assayers of mankind shall, in the holy presence of the Adored One, accept naught but absolute virtue and deeds of stainless purity. This is the day-star of wisdom and of divine mystery that hath shone above the horizon of the divine will. Blessed are they that turn thereunto.

70. O SON OF WORLDLINESS!

Pleasant is the realm of being, wert thou to attain thereto; glorious is the domain of eternity, shouldst thou pass beyond the world of mortality; sweet is the holy ecstasy if thou drinkest of the mystic chalice from the hands of the celestial Youth. Shouldst thou attain this station, thou wouldst be freed from destruction and death, from toil and sin.

71. O MY FRIENDS!

Call ye to mind that covenant ye have entered into with Me upon Mount Paran, situate within the hallowed precincts of Zaman. I have taken to witness the concourse on high and the dwellers in the city of eternity, yet now none do I find faithful unto the covenant. Of a certainty pride and rebellion have effaced it from the hearts, in such wise that no trace thereof remaineth. Yet knowing this, I waited and disclosed it not.

72. O MY SERVANT!

Thou art even as a finely tempered sword concealed in the darkness of its sheath and its value hidden from the artificer's knowledge. Wherefore come forth from the sheath of self and desire that thy worth may be made resplendent and manifest unto all the world.

73. O MY FRIEND!

Thou art the day-star of the heavens of My holiness, let not the defilement of the world eclipse thy splendor. Rend asunder the veil of heedlessness, that from behind the clouds thou mayest emerge resplendent and array all things with the apparel of life.

74. O CHILDREN OF VAINGLORY!

For a fleeting sovereignty ye have abandoned My imperishable dominion, and have adorned yourselves with the gay livery of the world and made of it your boast. By My beauty! All will I gather beneath the one-colored covering of the dust and efface all these diverse colors save them that choose My own, and that is purging from every color.

75. O CHILDREN OF NEGLIGENCE!

Set not your affections on mortal sovereignty and rejoice not therein. Ye are even as the unwary bird that with full confidence warbleth upon the bough; till of a sudden the fowler Death throws it upon the dust, and the melody, the form and the color are gone, leaving not a trace. Wherefore take heed, O bondslaves of desire!

76. O SON OF MY HANDMAID!

Guidance hath ever been given by words, and now it is given by deeds. Every one must show forth deeds that are pure and holy, for words are the property of all alike, whereas such deeds as these belong only to Our loved ones. Strive then with heart and soul to distinguish yourselves by your deeds. In this wise We counsel you in this holy and resplendent tablet.

77. O SON OF JUSTICE!

In the night-season the beauty of the immortal Being hath repaired from the emerald height of fidelity unto the Sadratu'l-Muntahá, and wept with such a weeping that the concourse on high and the dwellers of the realms above wailed at His lamenting. Whereupon there was asked, Why the wailing and weeping? He made reply: As bidden I waited expectant upon the hill of faithfulness, yet inhaled not from them that dwell on earth the fragrance of fidelity. Then summoned to return I beheld, and lo! certain doves of holiness were sore tried within the claws of the dogs of earth. Thereupon the Maid of heaven hastened forth unveiled and resplendent from Her mystic mansion, and asked of their names, and all were told but one. And when urged, the first letter thereof was uttered, whereupon the dwellers of the celestial chambers rushed forth out of their habitation of glory. And whilst the second letter was pronounced they fell down, one and all, upon the dust. At that moment a voice was heard from the inmost shrine: " Thus far and no farther."

Verily we bear witness to that which they have done and now are doing.

78. O SON OF MY HANDMAID!

Quaff from the tongue of the merciful the stream of divine mystery, and behold from the day-spring of divine utterance the unveiled splendor of the day-star of wisdom. Sow the seeds of My divine wisdom in the pure soil of the heart, and water them with the waters of certitude, that the hyacinths of knowledge and wisdom may spring up fresh and green from the holy city of the heart.

79. O SON OF DESIRE!

How long wilt thou soar in the realms of desire? Wings have I bestowed upon thee, that thou mayest fly to the realms of mystic holiness and not the regions of satanic fancy. The comb, too, have I given thee that thou mayest dress My raven locks, and not lacerate My throat.

80. O MY SERVANT!

Ye are the trees of My garden; ye must give forth goodly and wondrous fruits, that ye your-

selves and others may profit therefrom. Thus
it is incumbent on every one to engage in crafts
and professions, for therein lies the secret of
wealth, O men of understanding! For results
depend upon means, and the grace of God shall
be all-sufficient unto you. Trees that yield no
fruit have been and will ever be for the fire.

81. O MY SERVANT!

The basest of men are they that yield no fruit
on earth. Such men are verily counted as
among the dead, nay better are the dead in
the sight of God than those idle and worthless
souls.

82. O MY SERVANT!

The best of men are they that earn a livelihood
by their calling and spend upon themselves and
upon their kindred for the love of God, the Lord
of all worlds.

*The mystic and wondrous Bride, hidden ere this
beneath the veiling of utterance, hath now, by the
grace of God and His divine favor, been made
manifest even as the resplendent light shed by the
beauty of the Beloved. I bear witness, O friends!*

that the favor is complete, the argument fulfilled, the proof manifest and the evidence established. Let it now be seen what your endeavors in the path of detachment will reveal. In this wise hath the divine favor been fully vouchsafed unto you and unto them that are in heaven and on earth. All praise to God, the Lord of all Worlds.